Elegant Wedding Ceremonies

By Donna Kooler

A LEISURE ARTS PUBLICATION

10 9 8 7 6 5 4 3 2 1

Library of Congress Cataloging-in-Publication Data
     Kooler, Donna
     Elegant Wedding Ceremonies
     "A Leisure Arts Publication"

ISBN: 1-57486-207-3

Contributors

PRODUCED BY

PUBLISHED BY

If you have questions or comments
please contact:

LEISURE ARTS CUSTOMER SERVICE
P.O. Box 55595
Little Rock, AR 72215-9633
www.leisurearts.com

KOOLER DESIGN STUDIO, INC.
399 Taylor Blvd. Suite 104
Pleasant Hill, CA 94523
kds@koolerdesign.com

COLOR SEPARATIONS AND DIGITAL PREPRESS
AdMac, Emeryville, CA

PRINTED IN THE U.S.A. BY
R.R. Donnelley & Sons, Co.

KOOLER DESIGN STUDIO

PRESIDENT: Donna Kooler
EXECUTIVE V.P.: Linda Gillum
VICE PRESIDENT: Priscilla Timm
EDITOR: Judy Swager
ILLUSTRATORS: Linda Gillum, Barbara Baatz
Sandy Orton, Tom Taneyhill
Nancy Rossi, Jorja Hernandez
STAFF: Sara Angle, Jennifer Drake
Virginia Hanley-Rivett
Marsha Hinkson, Arlis Johnson
Karen Million, Char Randolph

ELEGANT WEDDING CEREMONIES

CREATIVE DIRECTOR: Donna Kooler
BOOK DESIGN: Nancy Wong Spindler
WRITERS: Kit Schlich, Shelley Carda
Joanne Lehrer
COPY EDITORS: Joan Cravens, Judy Swager
ILLUSTRATORS: Linda Gillum, Sandy Orton
PHOTOGRAPHERS: Dianne Woods, Berkeley, CA
Don Fraser, Berkeley, CA
PHOTO STYLISTS: Donna Kooler, Basha Hanner
Ina Rice
SUPPORT: Q. Stone Forbess, Laurie Grant
Dorene Kruspe
Deborah Magers-Rankin
Stephanie Podliska

With this ring . . .

Contents

THE PERFECT WEDDING FOR YOU.................... 7

DESIGNING YOUR WEDDING......................... 11

SENDING THE INVITATION.......................... 19

SETTING THE STAGE................................ 25

THE PERFECT FLOWERS............................ 39

BRIDAL ATTIRE 57

SPECIAL TOUCHES.................................. 75

CELEBRATING THE NEWLYWEDS.................... 83

Resources and Suppliers...................................... 90

Photo Credits 91

Index... 92

The Perfect Wedding For You

YOUR ENTIRE WORLD HAS CHANGED WITH ONE WORD: YES. With that single syllable you are ending an era, and about to begin a new one. It is an exciting prospect, full of promise and responsibility. How will you express your hopes for the future, and your journey from the past into that future?

Now that you have the happy task of planning a wedding, you will be called upon to make decisions regarding beauty, ritual, and meaning, as well as considering the prospect of feeding and housing dozens, maybe even hundreds of people.

We have designed this book to answer your questions about practical decisions, as well as to awaken you to the limitless possibilities for personal expression and creativity in the aesthetic and spiritual aspects of your wedding. With a balance of careful practicality and joyous abandon, you can have the wedding day of your dreams and your budget.

There it is. We have said the word: budget. You knew that it would come up sometime and that it might spoil all your fun. Well, it certainly doesn't have to. Of course it will limit your spending, but that has little to do with the beauty or elegance of your wedding. And it has even less to do with how much fun you have carrying off your wedding day in high style. That depends on how much creative thought and energy you put into the planning stage, and creative planning is most of the fun, at least up until the happy day itself.

The first step to enjoyable planning is to be organized. It is hard to make rational decisions if you must constantly hunt for little slips of paper or count on your fingers the days you have left. Design or purchase a calendar-style planning guide, and use it. Our companion book, the *Complete Wedding Guide* is a popular one. This will help you take notes and keep them together, so they are always accessible.

A bride and her attendants are the fairest flowers of all.

Tiny details, like family heirlooms, are the beginnings of family traditions.

Popular wedding and reception sites, photographers, and musicians are often booked a year in advance. If you want them, be prepared for a long engagement. If you are on a tighter schedule, do some detective work. Create a wedding, from invitations to the final toast, that is memorable because it is unique.

Should friends and family be enthusiastic about helping you with your wedding, welcome them. A loving gift of time and effort is worth far more in memories than a gift in a box.

Sewing, growing special flowers, making favors or appetizers, even moving chairs and putting up tents are wonderful gifts. It is a rare person who would be offended by hearing, "Your eye for arrangement is so good, I was wondering if for a wedding present you could help me set up the chairs on the lawn."

Select a beautiful location to save both time and money. Enough flowers can make a warehouse look like a cathedral, but is it worth it? You may do better with the cathedral. And if you have a perfect garden, have a perfect garden wedding.

The time when you have your reception has a bigger impact on your budget than what you serve. A wedding breakfast is less costly than a wedding dinner, and champagne punch is kinder to the guests (and the budget) than wine or cocktails. You also may get the services you want by scheduling your wedding before the afternoon rush.

Choosing alternatives can open lovely and unexpected vistas. If you must have a certain location or a service, you may get it if you schedule your wedding in the "off season." And sometimes the "season" is just one day:

A lush glade is an impressive setting, bright with summer flowers or in its own autumn glory.

Valentine's Day is more popular than Groundhog Day for just about everything.

Before you do anything else, sit down with your fiancé and discuss what the two of you want to express with your wedding. Write out the things which are important to you as a couple. Deciding what is meaningful to you will keep you from being tempted to spend money on someone else's idea of the perfect wedding. Someone else's wedding will look false to your guests and feel uncomfortable for you.

A wedding in which you can joyously express your beliefs in a personal way will be an intimate occasion to delight both you and the people who love you best. ॐ

Solemn vows and blessings give way to lighthearted frolics for the newlyweds.

Designing Your Wedding

PLANNING YOUR WEDDING IS CREATING A WORK OF ART. You will be the artist combining color, line, and the intangible qualities of your personality. It is your hand and spirit which will transform unrelated elements into a memorable visual and emotional composition.

Even if you have been dreaming of this day since you were six, when the time comes to translate your dreams into reality, you will turn fresh eyes on those dreams. Cherished fantasies of childhood may give way to new dreams of elegance and simplicity. Perhaps you now prefer a light labor of love to a complicated ceremony.

Your ceremony does not need to be complicated. A stately wedding can be had without enormous expense. A few fresh, beautiful flowers against a classic gown may be far lovelier for you than a huge bouquet and an elaborate dress. Likewise, a talented soloist performing a song of lyrical perfection in a small setting may be more suitable than an orchestra in a backyard garden.

Fitting all the pieces into the puzzle requires attention. As your preparations progress, take time frequently to consider the shape of things as a whole. A gown with a cathedral train may not fit into the tiny historic church you love. A bagpipe marching band may not be wildly popular at a sunrise garden wedding in the suburbs, although a single piper might. Taking the time to review the whole composition and refine the details before decisions have been set in stone will save you time, money, and disappointment.

PERSONAL TOUCHES: TRADITION, FAMILY, VOWS

Most cultures have ritualized the joining of a man and woman in matrimony. As nuptial customs have evolved, many now begin with a sacred ceremony and conclude with a secular celebration featuring food, drink, and (sometimes) dancing. Religious and ethnic traditions add grace, dignity, and significance to the ceremony.

Such traditions are rich in meaning to guests of that same ethnic background; this alone is sufficient reason to observe and honor them. The same traditions offer glimpses of a rare and unfamiliar culture to the other guests and can serve as a bridge to making friends of strangers. A nomadic heritage is recalled by the canopy or "chuppah" of the Jewish wedding, representing the roof of a couple's new home, which millennia ago was a tent in the Sinai desert. The honor shown to their ancestors by the Chinese is offered at a wedding by reverent bows to heaven and earth, to the ancestors, to the grandparents, and finally, to the groom's parents. A traditional Roman Catholic wedding is often celebrated with a High Solemn Nuptial Mass sung in Latin to centuries-old Gregorian chants, while the Russian Orthodox marriage liturgy is a three-hour-long Mass, sung while the congregation stands surrounding the crowned bridal couple.

Immigrants who strove to suppress their "foreign" ways in the new country now have children and grandchildren who seek to enrich this land with the deeply rooted customs of their ancestors. They often choose to recall in their weddings the ways of the old country. This is a lovely way to unite families across centuries and oceans and to bring the best of what is distant into our midst. The marriage of people from different backgrounds allows two cultures to mingle and blend their most joyous traditions. Planning for the ceremony may require exquisite tact and diplomacy, but if families are able to identify with the joy of a strong, shared love, the celebration can be a great success.

Rituals sometimes arise and quickly become traditions. Of recent origin is the lighting of a "unity candle" at the end of the ceremony, to signify the joining of two individuals into one. Though tradition rules much of the wedding, vows have become an area of individual expression. Some couples choose to use time-honored religious vows which define relationships and obligations. Some choose vows in archaic language to express the timelessness of their love. Still others prefer passages selected from favorite literary works to convey their hopes and promises for the marriage, or they compose their own profoundly personal vows. If you create completely original vows for the occasion, speaking the promises to your beloved by name will touch the hearts of all present.

Your wedding day is an occasion to unite the best of all traditions with that spark which is uniquely yours and, by the creation of your new family, to blend a rich past with your hopes for the future.

Wedding days are rich with tradition. Christian, Jewish, Buddhist, or modern secular culture, all societies solemnize marriage with beauty and grace.

DESIGNING WITH COLOR

Color is a subtle and powerful way to express emotions visually. Use your wedding color palette to reflect your sense of good taste and elegance.

Choose one color, with its tints and shades, to unify the visual impact of your wedding décor, or use several colors together to create visual harmony. Keep flowers, other decorations, attire, and invitations within this range. The colors you love are usually colors in which you look your best, so surround yourself with flattering colors.

When you have chosen a color scheme, take samples of the fabrics and flowers into the wedding and reception locations. Ambient or artificial light may change the most beautiful creamy yellow into mustard. Avoid unpleasant surprises.

Colors trigger emotional responses. Here are some basic ones to consider when choosing your colors:

RED—excitement, desire

ORANGE—energy, earthiness

YELLOW—joy, playfulness

GREEN—balance, calm

BLUE—sincerity, harmony

PURPLE—sensitivity, curiosity

The floral wreath (opposite), is actually a blossoming color wheel showing the relationship between the three primary colors—red, blue, yellow—and the three secondary colors—purple, green, orange. Notice the subtle changes that appear as each color blends into its neighbor.

Once you have at least one color in mind, choose the intensity. "Bright brights" such as the colors in the wreath, make a dramatic statement. Soft pastels are favorites for spring and summer. Muted ("grayed") pastels are lovely for romantic and vintage effects.

Different values of one color (a monochromatic scheme) are very effective. Do you want to add one or more accent colors? Explore the relationship between your chosen "signature" color and other colors on the wheel. Colors next to each other on the wheel (analogous) make attractive combinations. Colors that appear on opposite sides of the wheel (complementary) have the effect of bringing out the full essence of their opposites. Consider also a trio of colors: imagine a triangle connecting three colors on the wheel, such as green, purple, and yellow. You will find pleasing harmonies this way.

Fashion influences what colors are in style. If you pay attention to the colors currently shown in magazines and catalogs, you will not only gather new ideas, but also discover which colors will be easy to find as you plan the visual aspects of your wedding: ink and paper colors for your invitations, dresses for your attendants, decorations for both your ceremony and reception, bouquets and boutonnieres for your entire bridal party, favors and even your cake. ❧

SOFT PASTELS

BRIGHT BRIGHTS

MUTED PASTELS

Should You Use a Wedding Consultant?

A professional wedding consultant can help you plan and coordinate all aspects of your wedding, from the invitations to the getaway limousine, and everything in between. For this service a consultant charges an hourly fee or one based on a percentage of your wedding budget. You also can hire a consultant to coordinate only a portion of your wedding, such as the reception.

Does it make sense to hire a consultant? Yes, under certain circumstances. If you plan to marry in a city you do not currently live in, the right consultant will be a good investment. Also, planning a wedding can be time-consuming; if your schedule is so full that you lack the time to research wedding services to your satisfaction, a consultant may be a blessing.

If you choose to hire a consultant, seek word-of-mouth recommendations from satisfied brides as well as vendors such as photographers, bakers, florists, and caterers.

When interviewing a prospective consultant, ask for an explanation of his or her fee schedule. Find out how long the consultant has been in business; your chances for satisfaction are greater with an experienced consultant who has worked in your area for at least several years. Discuss how the consultant will accommodate your personal tastes. Ask how often he or she will communicate with you during the decision-making process. Above all, you must feel comfortable with the person who will make so many important arrangements for you.

Avoid individuals who advertise themselves as consultants but in reality want to sell you their own wedding and reception sites which you may not like. Conversely, if you find a site you like, you may elect to work with a site coordinator who can help you with a myriad of other wedding services. Such a set-up may prove cost-effective and free you from attending to all details yourself.

Once you've selected a consultant, be specific when discussing your budget. Determine during the initial interview whether the consultant listens to your preferences and tastes. Ask a consultant to explain in writing exactly what services you will receive and what the professional fee will be.

Romantic, Fun-loving, and Memorable Touches you can do...

Calligraphy unites the names of bride and groom in an emblem for invitations and other stationery.

A family pet—freshly groomed and spiffed up in wedding finery—awaits the guests' arrival.

✎ Select a personal emblem—a particular flower or tree, or some item of personal significance—and use it on invitations, wedding favors, and thank-you notes.

✎ Blend the initials of your name and your intended's into a new family crest, or have an artistic friend do the honor, and use it as your emblem on the above-mentioned items.

✎ When buying postage stamps for your invitations, choose the latest offering from the USPS's ongoing "Love" series.

✎ Wear your mother's or grandmother's wedding gown or jewelry.

✎ If you've chosen a historic home or inn for your ceremony, ask the site coordinator if you may accessorize tables and mantels using small framed photographs of you and your intended and your families, including wedding pictures of your parents.

✎ When writing your vows, include an anecdote about how you met each other.

✎ If you have a dog, and are planning an outdoor wedding, let your pet be part of the ceremony.

✎ If you and your intended are cycling enthusiasts, arrive at the ceremony on bicycles, either a matched pair or a tandem.

✎ Surprise your parents and grandparents during the ceremony by presenting each with a single rose that you've tucked behind your own floral spray. Include any children who will be part of this new family.

✎ If your marriage will create a blended family, invite the children—young or adult—to join hands at the end of the ceremony so the final blessing is bestowed on your entire new family.

✎ During your ceremony, have the officiant pause to remember friends and family members who are present only in memory.

✎ Ask the musicians to perform your favorite piece of music as the ceremony ends, even if it's unusual.

Mrs. Diane Koett
Mr. Ronald Koett
request the pleasure of your company
at the marriage of their daughter

Nicole Marie

to

Mr. Michael Gregory Blagden

Sunday, the twenty-second of August
Nineteen hundred and ninety-nine
at twelve o'clock
Piedmont Community Center
711 Highland Avenue
Piedmont, California

Reception immediately following the ceremony

Sending the Invitation

"…THE PLEASURE OF YOUR COMPANY IS REQUESTED."
Deciding with whom you would like to share your important day and requesting the "honor of their presence" brings the wedding one step closer.

An invitation provides a tantalizing clue to the style of your wedding. Let it hint at a wedding that is formal and traditional, opulently romantic, sleek and modern, or somewhere in between.

Traditional engraved invitations with black ink on white or ivory paper are elegant and appropriate for all but the most casual weddings. Companies specializing in wedding invitations now offer many variations from classically elegant to highly decorative.

Here are some other options besides commercially available invitations:

If you or your groom-to-be have expertise with computer-aided design, consider designing your own invitations. The creative possibilities are endless, with a vast array of attractive typefaces to choose from and the option of incorporating decorative artwork that has personal significance, such as your engagement photograph.

Do you have a family member or friend who is skilled in calligraphy? Ask him or her to design your invitation and provide a "master" that you can take to a printer, and hand-letter the addresses on the envelopes, too.

Wedding invitations can be individual without being casual. A hand-painted golden Chinese character signifying a loving and cherished friendship for eternity makes a touching and unusual invitation. A formal invitation in navy and gold features a distinctive border, while the traditional black-on-ecru adds whimsy with a cover sheet of rice paper and a frilly bow.

Blank museum-quality greeting cards or handcrafted paper with hand lettering are acceptable and make attractive keepsakes as well.

As you decide on the wording, indicate who is issuing the invitation, the names of you and your groom, the date, time, and location of the ceremony. If you are unsure of how to word your invitation, consult a wedding etiquette book or planning guide such as our companion book, the *Complete Wedding Guide*.

When should you mail your invitations? Six weeks before the wedding is customary. Send them earlier if the wedding falls on a holiday or long weekend or if you are inviting many out-of-town guests.

The gallery of contemporary invitations on the following pages shows the variety of papers available.

Invitations often include several enclosures designed in the same style as the invitation itself:

RECEPTION CARDS inform your guests that your reception is at a different location than the ceremony. These are especially important if only some, but not all, guests are invited to the reception. Avoid mentioning the reception on the invitation itself if you do not plan to include all the guests you invite to the ceremony.

RESPONSE CARDS are a courtesy that makes it simple for invited guests to let you know whether they plan to attend. Options include a small card with a pre-addressed, stamped envelope or a postcard.

MAPS to the ceremony and reception sites are a thoughtful touch if you think your guests will need directions. Also appreciated is a note to out-of-town guests, letting them know the name, address, and phone number of the hotel, motel, or bed and breakfast inn where you have arranged to have rooms set aside for your guests. These blocked rooms are usually held for a limited time, so let guests know the date by which they need to reserve their rooms to be sure of securing accommodations. ✣

A traditional black-on-ecru invitation with response card and decorative embossed border is always in good taste.

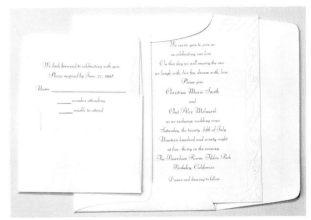

A contemporary invitation has a soft, romantic look thanks to the stylized script and handmade paper with flecks of dried flowers. The paper lines the inside of the envelope and wraps around the invitation. It is held in place by a vellum band. The return card tucks neatly under the band.

Another traditional invitation features lovely script on heavy paper stock with a gold edge. The decorative gold pattern of the envelope liner adds to the luxurious look.

White cardstock and green lettering give this invitation a fresh contemporary look. The delicate floral motif printed at the top of the invitation is repeated on the reception and reply cards, all printed on earth-friendly recycled paper.

A three-layer invitation is secured at the top with a lavender taffeta ribbon slipped through punched holes then tied into a bow. The top layer is vellum printed with the invitation; the second layer is a photo of the bride and groom which will show through the vellum; the third layer is a card inviting guests to the reception, with directions to the reception thoughtfully printed on the back.

This classic invitation, with its contemporary treatment of combined script and serif typefaces, is the epitome of elegance in its utter simplicity.

Another traditional invitation incorporating script and serif typefaces, with matching reception and direction cards, relies on its gold lettering for drama. The matching envelope is lined with gold paper.

Here, the names of the bride and groom in elegant gold script top a vellum cover over a gold-printed invitation combining script and serif typefaces.

TIPS FOR INVITATIONS

Printed invitations are available in many styles from a variety of sources: stationers, party stores, print shops, copy centers, mail order catalogs, and internet sites. Here are some tips to consider when placing your order.

✤ Use standard wording. Most printers follow the Crane Stationery company recommendations of wording style.

✤ Thermography printing is much less expensive than engraving.

✤ Large shapes and squares cost more and may require extra postage.

✤ Fewer enclosures will save money on both printing and mailing. For example, put the RSVP information on the reception card.

✤ Purchase an embosser with your address to emboss the back flap, and omit the printed return address.

✤ Count how many actual invitations you'll need, rather than the number of guests you're expecting; you may be inviting several guests with a single invitation. Order extra invitations and envelopes to allow for additional guests you may want to invite or for errors in addressing.

✤ When purchasing from a mail order catalog or the internet, request a sample so you can judge the quality of paper and printing. Or, to be safe, order a reputable name brand.

If your budget doesn't allow for some of the special touches you find in commercial invitation books, you may be able to achieve a similar effect with a small investment in time and energy. The simplest approach is to add a bow or translucent vellum cover to a standard printed invitation. Vellum paper is available from paper supply stores and mail order catalogs as well as craft stores (check the scrapbooking department). If you'd like to add a pretty bow, watch for sales on sheer or satin ribbon. Use about 12"-14" of ribbon per bow.

Computer-aided design, with a host of elegant typefaces and the ability to incorporate decorative artwork, offers numerous possibilities to anyone with a PC and applicable software. Using attractive paper and a laser printer, you can print as many invitations as you like. (When working with an ink jet printer, you may want to use a spray fixative for permanence.) Use conventional desktop-publishing programs, or purchase a wedding invitation software kit which includes the PC software as well as the card stock and envelopes. Additional invitations and accessory kits with ribbon and vellum are also available at craft or office supply stores.

Creating your invitations is fun, but when deciding to make them, keep in mind the number of invitations you'll need, the cost of supplies, and the time involved.

Setting the Stage

WEDDINGS ARE WONDERFUL CELEBRATIONS! YOURS WILL mark a joyful and significant change in your life, a new beginning, an affirmation of faith in the future. In the excitement of planning, it is fun to focus on the party aspects of the reception, but the exchange of vows lies at the heart of your wedding ceremony. You want the setting for your wedding to be pleasing, so unless you are happily tying the knot at city hall or in a judge's chambers, choose a location that appeals to your heart and to your aesthetic and spiritual preferences, too.

Once you and your intended have decided what style of ceremony you want and selected an officiant, the next step is to find a setting that matches the degree of formality, or informality, you desire. The time of year you select for your wedding plays a crucial role in your decision, as does the time of day. If you choose an outdoor setting, have a realistic and workable back-up plan in case the weather doesn't cooperate.

You also will want to consider the comfort of your guests. For example, will your beloved grandparents be able to negotiate a rocky beach setting? If you have your heart set on an unusual spot, it makes sense to limit your ceremony to only a few guests, perhaps immediate family or two witnesses. Hold the reception for any number of guests at another location later that day, or choose another reception date altogether. Make sure that transportation between the ceremony and reception will be easy for your guests and that parking and restroom facilities are available. For outdoor weddings, it's thoughtful to provide seating for all. Check municipal regulations if you choose a public place; some cities require a special license to hold a gathering such as a wedding.

A HOUSE OF WORSHIP, always a traditional choice for a wedding, appeals to many couples' spirituality. Choose the church you attended as a child, a rustic rural church, magnificent cathedral or synagogue, or small, intimate chapel. Is there a church whose architecture you've always admired? Perhaps the congregation will allow you to celebrate your wedding within its doors. Some religions require that the bride, groom, or both, be affiliated with that particular faith or congregation, so speak with the pastor or rabbi about this early in your wedding planning. Non-denominational churches may welcome non-members.

The expense of a house of worship may vary widely, especially if the location is in high demand for weddings. In all cases, expect to pay an officiant's fee along with a donation or small deposit for the establishment. Some religions and churches have restrictions on wedding elements such as music and photography; you will want to investigate these before making your decision.

HOTELS, RESTAURANTS AND CLUBS are often designed to accommodate large gatherings. Some specialize in weddings, offering packages of wedding services. These packages are often more economical than choosing the same elements yourself, on an a la carte basis. And a package will free you from having to attend to every detail on your own. As a bonus, you and your guests won't need to travel between the ceremony and the reception site.

A hotel or restaurant is a practical choice for an evening wedding or one held during the cooler months. A hotel ballroom or private dining room can be dressed up for a wedding with a simple arch and flowers.

From a soaring gothic cathedral to a dramatically lit wine cellar (opposite), there is a wedding setting to suit every personality and style.

A PRIVATE RESIDENCE has the appeal of familiarity and comfort. What could be simpler than getting married in the house you grew up in, with its precious memories? A beautiful fireplace, a dramatic staircase, a room with a panoramic view make appealing backdrops for your ceremony. Maybe one of your friends has a home with great architecture, a lush garden, backyard retreat, or that indefinable quality called "character." Think creatively! You may know someone with a yacht or vacation home who would be honored to provide you with your dream setting.

You may need to rent chairs and possibly a tent for an outdoor wedding. If you want to have your reception at the same location, determine whether kitchen facilities will be adequate.

HISTORIC HOMES, BED & BREAKFAST INNS, AND WINERIES with grand old architecture, precious antiques, and beautiful landscaping provide ambience for a romantic wedding. Check with the local historical society for possibilities. As with hotels and restaurants, many homes, inns, and historic sites offer a full package of services, including flowers and reception catering. Many have the option of both indoor and outdoor settings. Some homes may charge you a token deposit or use fee (in addition to charges for the wedding services package).

PARKS, PUBLIC GARDENS, RECREATION AREAS, AND BEACHES make beautiful and inexpensive settings. If you have your heart set on a themed wedding, or simply adore nature, the great outdoors offers unlimited choices, from the relative formality of a gazebo in a city park to the distinct informality of a sandy beach at sunset. Be sure to visit a prospective location at the same time of day you envision the wedding taking place, and inquire about the weather for the time of year.

Colorful paper parasols (below) ensure comfort on a sunny afternoon and make delightful favors for your guests.

Sleek contemporary interiors (above) are superb settings for a variety of wedding styles, from crisply modern to flawlessly traditional.

A wooded hillside (right) provides a breathtaking backdrop for an outdoor wedding and needs only a simple arch to focus all eyes on the exchange of vows.

Glorious rose bouquets and garlands, gossamer fabric draping, lacy ferns, and other live greenery create an elegant, romantic bower for this bride and groom.

DECORATIONS FOR THE CEREMONY

Weddings and flowers are inseparable. A bride without flowers welcoming her to the sacred space is unthinkable. The connection goes back to classical times, when the gods in charge of good fortune were invoked or thanked by wreaths and floral displays. This lovely and ancient tradition of demonstrating an abundance of blessings by the abundant beauty of nature has continued unbroken to modern times. The groom still buys his bride's bouquet, symbolizing his hopes, for his loved one. The bride's family pays for all other flowers.

INDOOR WEDDINGS do not need the entire floral produce of Holland to be lovely. Recognize the inherent beauty of your wedding spot. Church interiors are designed to be serenely beautiful. The ceremony takes place at the heart of the church, so flowers to soften the space and define your color scheme are all you need. A few of your favorite blooms, displayed to show the beauty of each, are more pleasing than a legion of gladioli.

If you have your wedding in a non-sanctified space, chances are you chose it because it is a lovely place to have a wedding. A few perfect flowers invite the eye to linger at the focal point until the bride arrives to claim the admiration.

MANTEL FLOWERS

For each arrangement, take a clean, bare 28-ounce can, and paint it the color you choose. Set the can on top of four 26"-square layers of tulle. Trim the corners round. One layer at a time, gather the tulle to the top, and finally tie all with a 45" length of ribbon. Add marbles for weight, a piece of oasis, and fresh or artificial flowers. We used white calla lilies and freesias.

How To Tie an Attractive Bow

TWO-LOOP BOW

1. Make equal-size loops on each side of the center of your ribbon.

2. Holding loops between thumbs and fore-fingers, cross right loop over left.

3. Keeping ribbon unbunched and untwisted, push right loop down behind left loop and up through the hole.

4. Hold the end of the loop in the hole and the left loop; pull to form bow. Adjust loops to desired length. Trim tails either on the diagonal or in an inverted "V."

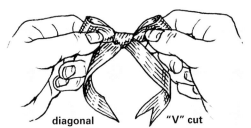

diagonal   **"V" cut**

SHOESTRING BOW

1. Make one loop to the left side of the center of your ribbon. Hold loop between thumb and fore-finger.

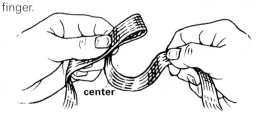

2. Wrap right ribbon length around loop without twisting ribbon.

3. Make a loop at the top of the ribbon length and insert through the wrap.

4. Hold the inserted loop end and the remaining loop; pull to form bow. Trim tails either on the diagonal or in an inverted "V."

Note: To make a bow on a wrapped object, first tie a left-over-right half knot—this becomes the center. Then proceed with either bow instructions.

center

A classically beautiful wreath on the front door promises joyful proceedings inside. This circle of silk flowers in white and lavender, with tendrils of ivy and a wired ribbon bow, is sure to become a treasured wedding memento in the new home.

Architectural elements (arches, stairs, and flower bedecked banisters) make this site perfect for an outdoor wedding.

With just a few chandeliers, an outdoor, tented wedding becomes a formal indoor space.

Rented, fern-filled urns, vine-wrapped arches, and portable flooring create an aisle in a garden.

OUTDOOR WEDDINGS should not need many additional flowers, since nature provides the settings that flowers imitate indoors. The seashore, a cottage garden, a forest glade, or a vista of fiery maples are already stunning backdrops. To direct the eye at an outdoor location, rent an arch and decorate it with tulle and ivy, leafy branches, or tiny white lights.

Consider using flowers from the wedding to decorate the reception, too. Vases of flowering quince, mums or lilacs can brighten the sanctuary and then the buffet or

bride's table. Display bridesmaids bouquets as decoration on the cake and punch tables while the ladies feast and dance away the night.

Stretch your flower budget by renting or buying trees, blooming shrubs, or topiaries from a plant rental shop or nursery. Shrubs such as azaleas or hydrangeas are available in five-gallon pots. Place them into inexpensive, decorative containers, embellishing them with moss above the soil. Then plant them in the garden, after the ceremony, as mementos of this special day.

Before the wedding, a friend drapes tulle over the back of the chairs and gathers it up with elastic and ribbon.

Wide wired ribbons tied in bows make simple but effective chair decorations (lower left).

(Lower right) The ring bearer and flower girl are all smiles as they join the wedding procession.

Decorate chairs or pews using generous lengths of inexpensive tulle, available by the yard or in rolls, just like ribbon. Tie it into fabulous bows, swag lengths from chair to chair, or wrap chairs individually, finishing your frothy creations with ribbon bows to soften and reflect your color scheme. ∽

A folding chair need not be just a folding chair. Tulle, bows, and ingenuity create graceful scarves and pinafores for gracious seating. Adding potted plants, (soon to be your garden!) creates a lovely floral entrance.

The Perfect Flowers

FLOWERS MAKE WEDDINGS BEAUTIFUL: THEIR SCENT, color, shape, and texture bring the Garden of Eden into a wedding. Allow your personality to shine through your choice of flowers and add an indescribable depth to routine floral wedding decorations. A bride in a tailored silk suit can reflect her delight in precise detail with a small, classic nosegay, or she can suddenly reveal her romantic personality to the world with a gloriously uninhibited bouquet of fragrant scarlet roses.

Whatever your secret floral passions, there should be a certain harmony to the flowers at a wedding. If your wedding is wildly romantic, with the rustle of silk and clouds of tulle everywhere, then the bouquets and the other flowers should look completely at home, both with the surroundings and with each other. For the bride to carry rare orchids but decorate her table with dried milkweed pods would look silly if not jarring.

A word about weeds. A weed is any plant growing where you don't want it. If your personality cries out for wild cornflowers and Queen Anne's lace, then by all means have them. The fact that a flower grows in a field without a lot of fuss doesn't make it less beautiful. Beauty is everywhere, and choosing the flowers that you love best will make the loveliest bouquet for you.

In addition to flowers, extra touches in your bouquet add glimpses into your imagination. Keeping your bridal colors in mind, you might add pinecones, velvet leaves, heirloom lace, seashells, or ribbons to enhance and personalize your bouquet. For an evening wedding, consider embellishing the bouquet using sparkling crystal sprays or a handle wrapped with faux jewels. A lace handkerchief around the stems of wildflowers places a meadow in your hand.

If you are marrying in a garden, coordinate your wedding decorations with the flowers that will be in bloom, so they look like they have been spontaneously plucked from the border. Should you marry at an historic site with established gardens, let your flowers be a lovely visual allusion to the surroundings. Lush green locations, such as parks or lakesides, are inviting backgrounds for whatever flowers you love.

Think about the fragrance of your bouquet as well. The subtle scent of lavender or the spicy fragrance of carnation sets a mood and may calm your jitters as you walk down the aisle. A few sprigs of herbs such as mint or rosemary add a refreshing note. If you have a favorite perfume, ask your florist to help you find its basic floral component, then carry a bouquet of flowers with a similar fragrance.

SINGLE-FLOWER BOUQUETS

Single-flower bouquets are favorites, since many flowers are most effective when massed and bound simply with a ribbon. Gentle lily-of-the-valley, demure violets, or vibrant day lilies are all superb on their own.

You can create the mood of any bouquet simply by the way you wrap the stems: a dressy bouquet with the stems in satin ribbon secured with pearl-tipped corsage pins, or stems woven with raffia or twine for a more casual look. Single-flower bouquets, saturated with color, look wonderful with slim-silhouetted dresses. The smallest bloom of the bunch makes a tidy boutonniere.

A dome of roses, tightly packed and rich with fragrance, is a modern single-flower classic. Beautiful in any season and flattering to any bride, it is aesthetically and economically balanced by bridesmaids carrying a single rose with long, graceful streamers.

Even the most traditional bride has an unconventional side. Reveal your dual nature by your bridesmaids' outfits and flowers.

Simple modern gowns are even more interesting when paired with nature's best.

In a prim pink bouquet (left) or massed in several subtle tints (above), roses compliment many bridal styles.

SEIZE THE DAY

Of course, white roses are always appropriate, but there is such a riot of colorful flowers at hand that it is hard not to burst out in rainbows. Try blending your bouquets not only with the season, but also with the time of day. Morning weddings beg for the tender colors of sweet peas at dawn. Vivid dahlias are even brighter in August sunsets. Fall's brilliant afternoons gild the tips of asters, and make a kaleidoscope of chrysanthemums. Icy winter days reflect beautifully on silvery lavender or heather blended with cool greens. Chilly holiday evenings suggest twining holly and bright ivy with wine-red blooms. Bathe your wedding with the colors of the hour and rejoice.

Tightly packed domes of roses in sorbet colors (above) are a perfect choice for warm summer weddings and a perfect foil for the bride's roses in creamy white (opposite).

A mixed flower bouquet is an armful of beauty, with a multitude of flowers and graceful vines.

MIXED BOUQUETS

Mixed bouquets allow you to blend local seasonal flowers with imported varieties. Mix roses with your own white lilacs and new ivy for a spring bouquet hinting at summer. Or choose daffodils and spiky Siberian iris for a winter bouquet so bright it practically melts the snow. And a delicate bouquet of yarrow and field clover smells of sun-warmed honey.

Fragrant herbs are as versatile, but less well known than flowers. Tuck sprigs in bouquets to hint at aroma, or be bolder and make coronets for your attendants. Rosemary for remembrance, sage for wisdom, thyme for courage, and mint for virtue are traditional choices. Fresh herbs are as close as your grocery produce section.

Fresh herbs are available year 'round, so an herbal bouquet is an excellent choice anytime.

THE LANGUAGE OF FLOWERS

The Victorians developed a complex language of flowers, assigning to each flower a hidden meaning. A suitor could express his love with a single flower or send a complex message in a mixed bouquet. Fond thoughts in these floral greetings were not restricted to lovers—a woman might send a close friend or relative a nosegay to show her affection. Today using this language is a romantic and fun way to create your bouquet. Here are a few flowers as suggestions.

Amaranth—unfading love

Beech—prosperity

Calla lily—elegance

Chestnut—luxury

Cape jasmine—transport of joy

Four-leaf clover—be mine

Forget-me-not—true love

Oak-leafed geranium—true
    friendship

Heliotrope—devotion

Honeysuckle—bonds of love

Ivy—fidelity

Lemon blossoms—fidelity

Lily-of-the-valley—sweetness

Primrose—first love

Purple lilac—first emotions of
    love

Single pink—pure love

Spring crocus—youthful
    gladness

Sweet pea—lasting pleasures

White rose—only for thee

White and red roses—unity

Red sage—forever yours

Veronica—fidelity

Violet—innocent love

Wheat stalk— riches, fertility

Zinnia—thoughts of absent
    friends

CALLA BOUQUET

First, gather 20 callas in your hand, building an outward spiral from a single bloom and placing each flower point out. Secure with rubber band or twine. Wrap the stems with florist's tape, and trim ends even (Step 1, opposite).

For the wrapped handle; from a 1¾" yard of 2"-wide double-faced satin, cut 6" and 9" lengths. Center the 6" length over stem bottoms and hot-glue ribbon to sides (Step 2). Using the remaining 48" length, measure up 4" from bottom of handle and hot-glue ribbon end in place diagonally. Beginning at the bottom, wrap stems spiraling up to the base of flowers; leave a 4" tail (Step 3). Thread tail under bottom edge of top wrap and out at top. Pull up ribbon tightly at a diagonal. Secure with a corsage pin. Trim end diagonally using pinking shears.

For the looped bow: using a 9" length of ribbon, wrap a loose loop around thumb, holding it in place with forefinger. On either side of loop, form two equal loops, tucking end directly under center thumb loop. Attach bow at the top of stem handle with three corsage pins down the center loop (Step 4).

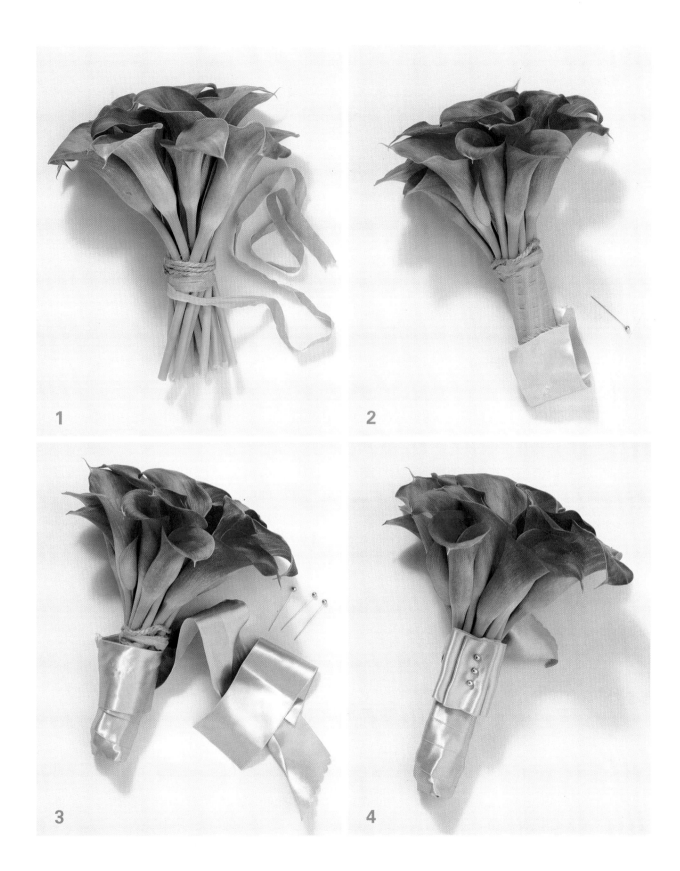

1

2

3

4

Alternatives to bouquets include carrying a prayer book adorned with a single flower, wearing beautiful flowers in your hair, walking down the aisle with Fido on a beribboned leash, or, for a winter wedding, carrying a spray of flowers with trailing silver ribbons pinned to a faux fur muff.

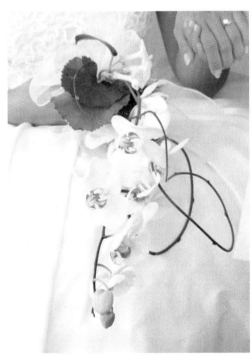

Orchids are classic wedding flowers, perfect for adorning the head or gracing the hand. Try a spray tucked up in your hair, or a few perfect blooms on a bible or prayer book.

WORKING WITH A FLORIST

Your florist can help you turn your dream wedding into a reality. The cost of flowers takes up about six percent of your total wedding expenses, so this is an excellent place to economize.

First, interview several florists. You can sense the florist's style by looking around the shop and perusing the shop's portfolio. Does the florist make standard bouquets, or are there extra touches that make them special? Does the florist's style match your own? If the shop is filled with dramatic tropical arrangements and you're looking for simple cornflowers and cosmos, then look elsewhere. Your florist should be happy to work within your budget, so be candid about what you are willing to spend. Remember, too, when estimating costs, you are paying for the florist's time and skill as well as the flowers. Anyone can make a dozen roses beautiful, but an artist can make field flowers just as lovely without breaking the bank.

You might also consider a less traditional florist. Why not the one at the grocery store, if you have ever admired the flowers on your way to the salads? Other floral artists work out of their homes and have less overhead than a shop. If you see magnificent bouquets at the farmers' market, ask the vendor if they do weddings. Or have a florist make bouquets, boutonnieres, and corsages, and ask a friend to do the other floral arrangements.

Your florist will also be able to offer advice on the availability of seasonal flowers. Although the flowers themselves are only part of the cost, local and seasonal flowers may be less expensive. If you're getting married on Valentine's Day, you'll save money but still have a dramatic bouquet with a packed dome of crimson carnations rather than red roses. Any flowers can be stunning when arranged with an artful eye.

The number of flowers you need affects the cost as well. Bouquets for the bride and her attendants and boutonnieres for the groom and groomsmen are essential; corsages for the mothers are a thoughtful touch. Look carefully at your ceremony and reception settings. Where will your guests be spending their time? Put your flowers in those places (and at the entrance to the location) so guests can enjoy them.

SEASONAL FLOWERS

When selecting your wedding flowers, think local and seasonal—they will be fresher and less expensive than imported ones. For example, consider peonies in the springtime if you live in Kansas, delphiniums in California. The following list is meant as a general guide, and seasons will overlap. For example, tulips are available in winter, but become most abundant (and therefore less expensive) in the spring.

SPRING	SUMMER	AUTUMN	WINTER	ALL YEAR
Anemone	Artichoke	Amaranth	Amaryllis	Alstroemeria
Clematis	Bells of Ireland	Aster	Clematis (seed	Asters
Colombine	Campanula	Berries	heads)	Baby's breath
Crocus	Cornflower	Chinese lantern	Curly hazel	Bells of Ireland
Daffodil	Cosmos	Colchicum	Curly willow	Calla
Euphorbia	Delphinium	Dahlia	Cyclamen	Carnation
Hyacinth	Hollyhock	Decorative leaves	Daphne	Chrysanthemum
Lilac	Honeysuckle	(oak, maple etc.)	Evergreens	Delphinium
Lily-of-the-valley	Iris	Gladiolus	Flowering quince	Dianthus
Magnolia	Lady's mantle	Helenium	Hellebore	Dried flowers
Narcissus	Lavender	Japanese anemone	Jasmine	Eucalyptus
Peony	Lily	Nicotiana	Mistletoe	Freesia
Poppy	Lupin	Nerine	Olive	Gardenia
Primrose	Marigold	Ornamental pepper	Pansy and viola	Gerbera
Pussy willow	Sea holly	Penstemon	Paperwhite	Ivy
Ranunculus	Snapdragon	Rudbeckia	narcissus	Rose
Sweet pea	Sunflower	Smokebush	Snowdrop	Snapdragon
Tulip			Witch hazel	Statice
Viburnum				Stephanotis

Mix silk leaves and fresh flowers for something rare and spectacular. Here blushing faux grapes blend with bronze callas for a bouquet to warm an autumn evening.

Boutonnieres, from left: calla lily with scented geranium leaf, white and yellow rosebuds, and an apricot rose.
Center: a sprig of snowberries, three single hydrangea blossoms, hellebore and acorns.
Bottom: lavender and oregano with lamb's ear, lily-of-the-valley and dusty miller with a slender leaf.

BOUTONNIERES AND CORSAGES

Boutonnieres and corsages are designed to distinguish the wearers. They are presented to the groomsmen, parents, close relatives, and friends of the bridal couple. The tendency has been to make them all as similar as possible, but this is not really necessary. All that matters is that the corsages be pretty. In fact, ladies rather like being unique.

Corsages for the mothers are chosen specifically to accent their dresses. This means that the florist should be shown either the dresses or fabric samples as far in advance of the wedding as possible. It is wise to label the mothers' corsage boxes so that no unfortunate mix-up occurs. If you are giving corsages to other ladies, it is safest to design them to complement any color dress. White flowers go with everything. Bright coral roses may not.

Clockwise from left: violas mixed with lily-of-the-valley, lavender, and oregano; snowberries, hellebore, and orchids in a wrist corsage, a bag pinned with roses, callas, herbs and more.

Don't be afraid of color in a boutonniere; liven up the groom's side of the group to balance the composition.

Ask the recipient if she would prefer a wrist or purse corsage to a traditional pinned corsage, since these arrangements will not damage clothing. Consider a gift of a tiny handbag with flowers attached. Whatever you choose is sure to be appreciated as a token of your affection. It will make the wearer feel appreciated at this important moment in your life.

The boutonnieres usually coordinate with the brides-maids' or the bride's bouquets, but there is no fixed rule about which particular flower to use. If you have several different kinds of flowers in the bouquets, consider making all the boutonnieres different. The bridesmaids may even spend a day of fun designing and making individual boutonnieres. A single small bloom or spray and perhaps an attractive bit of green are enough. In any case, keep them small and understated. ☞

How To Care
for Your Flowers

To continue looking their best, flowers require conditioning. Off the plant, they still need food and water to survive. If a florist is arranging your flowers, he or she will have conditioned them before making your bouquets and floral decorations. If you are buying from a flower mart, farmers' market, or even picking them from your garden, condition them before arranging. (This is the perfect task to give relatives or friends who want to help just before the wedding.) Don't be tempted to skip this step— properly conditioned flowers will look livelier and last much longer. To condition like the pros, clean buckets, clean water, floral food, and a selection of sharp scissors, knives, or clippers are essential.

Gallon-size plastic buckets are widely available. Avoid metal, because flower food will discolor both the bucket and stems of the flowers. Scrub your buckets with soap and water. Add floral food to the bucket, then the water. Groom the flowers before adding them to the bucket: separate the bunches, remove all leaves that will go below the water line, then re-cut the stems at a 45-degree angle. As soon as you cut the flowers, plunge them into the water, and leave them in a cool, dark place such as a garage or basement for several hours or overnight. If you want rose buds or other tight flowers to open quickly, add some "bud opener" to the water.

When you are ready to arrange your flowers, add a scoop of flower food to each vase. Fill with tepid water, then build your arrangement, stem by stem.

Love is elegantly accompanied by this rose and hydrangea bouquet (right).

Bridal Attire

WHEN YOU ENVISION YOUR IDEAL WEDDING IT'S LIKELY YOU picture yourself in a gown that makes you look and feel beautiful. Since all eyes will be on you throughout the day—standing, bending, dancing, or throwing a bouquet—you want to be as lovely and comfortable as possible. Choose a gown that is flattering, easy to move in, and well made.

Despite changes in wedding fashion and formality, some things do not change. One of these is the cut of classic gowns. These styles are classics because they always look good. A particular style may not be right for every body type, but the style is never dated.

This does not mean that tastes do not change. Some decades are full of tulle, ruffles, and crinolines, such as we saw after the wedding of Princess Diana. Some decades are A-line and tailored, as were the '60s. But in every decade you can find dresses in all of the classic shapes, all completely fashionable. What makes wedding fashion is the color, type of fabric, or trim. Peau de soie may be more fashionable than beaded Alençon lace, though the cut of the gowns is identical. The delight is in the details.

You may prefer to wear a period gown. If so, choose an original, have a dressmaker copy made, or create one of your own.

Dress as the bride of your dreams in a gown as romantic and sumptuous as you wish.

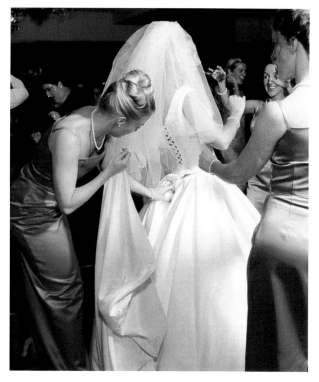

Bridesmaids "attend" to the bride's gown, one of their traditional roles as helpers on the special day.

YOUR BRIDAL GOWN

What do you want in a gown? As you think about the elements that are most important to you, including matching your dreams to your budget, here are some considerations.

WEATHER OR NOT

Whatever style of gown you choose, there is a way to "season" it. A skirt and crinoline worn with a boned bodice of heavy satin would be stifling in July. The same style in batiste will be cooler in high summer.

Winter is ideal for warm velvets and heavy brocades. A plunging back or sleeveless bodice may need a small jacket or scarf. Consider religious restrictions, too. Many sanctuaries forbid bare arms or shoulders, so inquire before you choose a dress.

Rules about formal versus casual have relaxed somewhat, but there are still practical and aesthetic considerations. Long trains have inconveniences that may outweigh their beauty. To appear to advantage, a long train needs a lot of space to move gracefully, and lots of bridesmaids to move it. Even if the train can be hooked up for dancing, practice climbing stairs and entering and leaving cars gracefully. While white or black tie is not critical, outdoor weddings and receptions are more easily navigated in shorter gowns.

BALANCING FLOWERS

Your gown is not just a work of art; it is the backdrop for a work of art. Use it to balance or to set off your bouquet, depending on the effect desired. A sleek modern gown will enhance a simple dome bouquet or showcase any large bouquet, bright or monochromatic. An elaborate gown balances an elaborate bouquet of red roses, but makes a single rose look insignificant, and it might make a large multi-hued bouquet look like a jumble. Strive for an elegant equilibrium.

When Judy Bretz wed Douglas Swager in 1969, she chose a lovely dress custom made for her diminutive size 2 figure.

A contemporary white suit with lacy details was this bride's choice for a wedding at an elegant winery.

DOES BRIDAL MEAN WHITE?

In less prosperous times a white dress, used only once for a wedding, was extravagant. If people did indulge in a special white dress, it was handed down to the next generation and beyond, to justify the expense. Heirloom dresses are lovely examples of a living tradition.

White has long been the color of purity and virginity, though it wasn't synonymous with wedding dresses until Queen Victoria set the trend in 1840. While other cultures have their own traditional wedding costumes, often red, a long white dress is now the wedding garment of choice in many countries. For the traditional wedding, a white gown is almost an absolute. Suits, cocktail dresses, and other garments crisply tailored in white are often the choice of brides whose personal style is more chic than romantic.

Of late, some brides have worn the palest pastels for traditional weddings. If you find that no shade of cream or white flatters you, then the pastel range may be just what you seek. Distinction between bridesmaid and bride is maintained by flowers, headdress, and, of course, by the groom.

Gowns other than the traditional wedding gown are also popular. Evening gowns cut and decorated along distinctly non-bridal lines are a practical alternative to the white dress.

There is a beautiful gown for every budget. An exclusive bridal shop will have matching prices. A talented seamstress can copy anything, but even the fabrics may cost more than you want to spend. Check out gown rentals, thrift shops, classified ads, and ask your friends if anyone has a gown to lend. You may find what you love, and have it altered, for much less than you had budgeted for a new dress.

Princess

Cap or off-the-shoulder sleeve

Sweetheart neckline

Semi-fitted waist

Full flared skirt

Short "chapel" train

Lace appliqué accents

Medium "cathedral" detachable train

Sheath

Spaghetti straps

Empire

Square neckline

Sheer puffed sleeve

Shawl instead of train

Slim skirt with sheer tiered overskirt

Column shaped skirt

FASHION SAVVY

To help you discuss your gown with a salesperson or dressmaker, here's a guide to basic style elements.

SILHOUETTES are influenced by the size and sweep of the skirt as well as by the waistline treatment, which may or may not be defined at all. Numerous combinations of these two features create a variety of silhouettes. Some of these design elements may be combined; for example, an empire style may feature a princess-seamed bodice and a sheath-like skirt. Nevertheless, it's possible to make some generalizations about basic silhouettes and the figure types they flatter.

PRINCESS STYLE achieves shaping through vertical seams and may or may not have a waistline. Often featuring a flared skirt, this traditional favorite offers a timeless bridal look.

❧ Flattering for every figure and every height

Basque Waist

Leg o'mutton sleeve

"V" neck

Full gathered skirt attached to a drop waist

Long "sweep" train

Unstructured

Scoop neckline

Flounced cuff

Loose raised waistline

Ballroom

Strapless boned bodice

Irregular hem—sheer overskirt

Optional "illusion" with satin edging

Fitted sashed waist

Full gathered multi-tiered skirt

SHEATH STYLE is slim and columnar, achieving its shaping through darts or, for the perfect figure, a bias cut. Often without a waistline or sleeves, it offers a contemporary and sophisticated look.

❧ Flattering on all heights

❧ Camouflages a figure without a defined waist

❧ May emphasize large hips or thighs

EMPIRE STYLE, with a waistline raised to just under the bustline, imparts a youthful look, and can be contemporary or vintage, depending on details. The skirt may be flared or columnar.

❧ Flattering on an average figure of any height

❧ Camouflages a thick waist

❧ May not be a good choice for heavy-busted figures

BALL GOWN, a traditional, popular bridal style, has a fitted bodice and waistline, with a full skirt. It may be strapless, sleeveless, or with sleeves of any length.

❧ Flattering on a figure with a defined waist, as well as a figure with large hips or thighs

❧ May overpower a petite figure

BASQUE WAIST (also called "princess waist," not to be confused with princess style mentioned above) is similar to a ball gown silhouette, but has an elongated (dropped) fitted bodice that comes to a point or curved dip at center front, creating a romantic look.

❧ Flattering on a figure with a defined waist, as well as a figure with large hips or thighs

❧ May overpower a petite figure

UNSTRUCTURED may include layers or "floats" of sheer fabric(s) and may be asymmetrical, of any length, and designed with trims or interesting hem details. Provides a wispy, ethereal look.

❧ Camouflages a thick waist and other figure flaws

TIP: It's likely that your guests will be looking at the back of your gown during the ceremony. Look for a gown with interesting dressmaker details, rather than a utilitarian "zip up the back."

BRIDAL DRESSMAKING TERMS

SWEEP is the circumference of the gown's hem, which directly affects the silhouette, whether narrow for a sheath or voluminous (three feet or more) for a full skirt.

TRAIN is that portion of the gown's back hem that trails on the floor. A gown may have a built-in or detachable train. Some built-in trains have loops at the back hem that allow you to drape ("bustle-up") the train off the floor. Detachable trains are removable for dancing.

BUSTLE is concentrated fullness in the back of the skirt and may include an additional pouf or draped layer for more fullness. It imparts a sumptuous, vintage touch.

A dramatic scoop, intricate beadwork, and a family heirloom brooch add back interest to this gown.

TIERS are additional, often sheer, layers of skirt attached at the waist in graduated lengths, or a skirt with multiple horizontal seams, each one with more fullness than the one above it.

FLOUNCE is a deep ruffle that may appear at the bottom of the gown or at a dropped neckline (draping over the arms) for a romantic look.

ILLUSION is sheer fabric at bodice or sleeve giving the illusion of bareness yet providing a foundation for an added lace collar, cuffs, or scattered motifs.

BONING is flexible plastic reinforcement that maintains shape in a snugly fitted, often strapless, bodice.

SHOPPING AT A BRIDAL SALON

Your visit to a bridal salon provides an opportunity to try on a variety of styles. You may discover the perfect dress for you. Certainly by trying on a variety of gowns you can explore your style preferences.

The most expensive bridal gowns purchased at a bridal salon are made to order. Less expensive gowns are made in standard sizes, then altered to fit. They have less ease than casual ready-to-wear clothing. Make sure a salesperson takes your measurements. If your measurements span two sizes, discuss with the alterations specialist which size to order. Altering the bust may be harder than altering the hips or waist, unless you are wearing a sheath. Check with a seamstress to be sure.

Allow three months or more for completion of a custom gown. You'll likely want last-minute adjustments in fit, so schedule the "due date" for your gown well before your big day.

SELECTING A USED OR PERIOD GOWN

Many bridal shops sell beautiful gowns already worn by another bride for only a day. They're worth a look and can offer your budget substantial savings.

If you are interested in a genuine period gown, be aware that the sizing of period fashions is quite different

An heirloom gown can connect generations of happy brides.

from modern standard sizing, and radical alterations may be necessary. Modern undergarments also change the way dresses fit. Make sure the fabric is sound enough to withstand cleaning and altering. All in all, it may be easier to copy a period gown than to alter the original.

The Ingenue—Shaping the bodice and adding a tulle skirt transforms a sheath dress into bridal finery.
Sophisticated Lady—A sheer, finely trimmed bolero jacket dresses up a basic sheath dress.

MAKING YOUR OWN CUSTOM GOWN

Making your gown is a rewarding choice that gives you total control over style and fit. Perhaps you or someone in your family is adept at sewing or designing. Or, you might work with a professional dressmaker to develop your gown, whether you begin from scratch (with a pattern or not) or revamp an existing gown.

If you're a savvy shopper, another option is to look for a basic dress to transform into your dream gown. That's exactly what we did with a simple floor-length, sleeveless, semi-fitted ivory sheath dress which we found for $59.99 at a local outlet store. We bought two identical dresses to show you two dramatically different ways they could be personalized. Our adept dressmaker worked her magic, and you can duplicate her effort at home.

GOWN 1—THE INGENUE

We set out to completely transform the silhouette from slim and columnar to hourglass-shaped with a full skirt. To achieve this, the dressmaker added multiple sheer layers of inexpensive bridal illusion (tulle) for a ballerina skirt. She chose four layers, but you could add more if you want a more bouffant look.

First our dressmaker fitted the bodice snugly to the bride's figure, the better to complement the full skirt. Next she determined where the new dropped-waist seam should fall for maximum flattery. To accentuate the ballerina look, she reworked the neckline by rounding it and scooping it deeper.

She cut four large rectangles of tulle for the overskirt, gathered them to fit the waist, then re-sewed the bodice to the now multi-tiered skirt. The final touch was to finish the edges of the top two tiers of tulle with narrow satin ribbon, simply topstitching it above the raw edge, then trimming the tulle even with the ribbon.

The ballerina bride is now ready for a romantic dance with her groom.

GOWN 2—SOPHISTICATED LADY

For this completely different look we scarcely touched the basic dress, making only minor adjustments to achieve a perfect fit. Our dressmaker added a bolero jacket of utterly simple cut, using inexpensive polyester organza, a fabric firm enough to support the added braid trim. It was easy to find a pattern for a straight, simple jacket, then shorten it for the classic bolero style.

The dressmaker created the jacket trim from an assortment of inexpensive, easy-to-find braid. To reproduce this treatment, look for braid that can handle curves easily without buckling. Topstitch the rows of braid in place after constructing the bolero, curving and looping individual pieces into a design fantasy.

Simplicity of line and fabulous detail make a stunning, sophisticated statement.

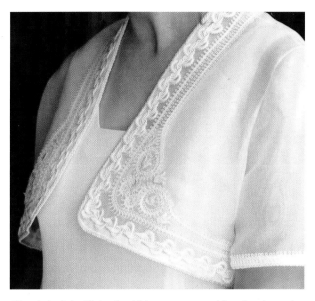

Topstitched braid in fanciful patterns provides the decorative accent on a simple bolero jacket.

WORKING WITH A DRESSMAKER OR SALESPERSON

❧ Be prepared to spend some time; zeroing-in on your perfect gown is a happy task that should not be rushed.

❧ Bring lots of photos or sketches (or both) to demonstrate the silhouettes and details you like.

❧ If you work with a dressmaker, realize that your gown will be a joint creation.

❧ Whether you work with a dressmaker or shop at a bridal salon, always wear the same undergarments you plan to wear on your wedding day, as well as shoes with the same heel height.

❧ At fittings, avoid wearing makeup that may soil the dresses as you take them on and off.

❧ Ask about how many fittings you should expect, and the cost of alterations.

SOMETHING BORROWED...

Borrowing a bridal gown can be an appealing choice, especially if the gown was once worn by a close family member. What better tribute to your mother than wearing her gown? You may need to make adjustments, perhaps even alter some of the design elements, to ensure an accurate and attractive fit.

Bridal finery handed down through generations acquires sentimental value, as the following story reveals.

Mayme Bloch Russakov wore this exquisite lace veil with bonnet at her 1914 wedding. It remains in the family and is now under the care of a niece.

Some families have lovely wedding gowns which have been worn by generations of brides, who are honored to carry on the tradition. The Wakeland Family gown is one of these beloved heirlooms.

Mary Jane Wakeland purchased this elegant ivory satin gown with voluminous train for $75 in 1942, with the understanding that her younger sister, Cathleen Ann Wakeland, would eventually wear the gown.

Cathleen Ann Wakeland became the second bride to wear the gown when she married in 1946. Cathleen chose a long veil with a train to echo the gown's dramatic train.

The third bride was Bonnie Case Harris, a friend of the Wakeland sisters, who wore the gown in 1951. Little is known of the fourth and fifth brides to wear the gown other than they were daughters of friends of the Wakeland family.

For 25 years the gown languished in closets of both Wakeland sisters until it was rediscovered in 1980. The daughter of Cathleen Wakeland Stone, Cathy Ann (above left), became the sixth bride to wear the gown at her wedding in 1980. Her pillbox hat was covered with satin taken from fabric of the train (thus shortening the train somewhat).

Keely Hubbard (above right), the daughter of Mary Jane Wakeland Hubbard (the original bride) wore the gown at her wedding in 1983. She is now the gown's caretaker and speaks for her generation: "The gown is a treasure that keeps us close to our late mothers, and we feel we each have a real part of them for as long as we live."

A happy marriage! The Wakeland family's gown and the Russakov lace veil blend together beautifully with their color match and equally dramatic lengths. Because the style lines of the gown are simple and timeless, its appeal will never wane. Beautiful lace is able to transcend the caprices of fashion. Both heirlooms are ready to be worn by a new generation of brides.

The veil surrounds a bride in a halo of light and lace.

This swept-back veil attached to a delicate coronet is simple to make and elegant in any setting.

THE BRIDAL HEADPIECE

Our custom of wedding veils comes from the Romans, who covered brides with saffron-colored veils to keep away bad luck. The fact that the veil also kept brides and grooms from seeing the mates chosen for them by matchmakers was just coincidence.

Whether it's a frothy pouf of tulle, a rhinestone tiara, a wreath of flowers, or a simple silk ribbon rose, your headpiece will be the crowning touch to your wedding day attire, framing your happy face and defining you as a bride, perhaps even more than your gown will.

Before choosing a style for your headpiece, decide how you want to style your hair on your wedding day. Either your hairstyle will be the most important element, or your headpiece will be. You will want to make sure your hairstyle and headpiece harmonize beautifully—avoid setting a hat atop an elaborate updo.

Ready-to-wear bridal headpieces are costly because they are fragile and labor intensive. Yet even highly decorative headpieces can be easy and inexpensive to make yourself. A handcrafted headpiece offers you the opportunity for a unique personal expression.

You can easily make a two-tier veil as shown in the illustrations, opposite. Wear the top tier (sometimes called a "blusher") forward over your face or to the back, topping the second tier.

When shopping for fabric, look for bridal-quality tulle, also called "bridal illusion," in white or ivory. Select a width of 45 to 108 inches depending on the fullness you desire. Buy an amount equal to the length of both tiers and add another half yard for the "pouf," which shortens the length. If you're unsure, buy more than you think you need; tulle is inexpensive and you can always trim any excess.

Headpieces may include inexpensive headbands and tiaras, which you can find in the accessory department of your favorite store. For traditional elegance, attach your hand-made veil.

Flowers have a long tradition as bridal hair ornaments. Queen Victoria made orange blossoms the rage by wearing a coronet of orange blossoms at her wedding. You can continue the custom by making your own coronet of small silk or fresh flowers with a bit of wire and floral tape.

You may prefer a single flower or a small cluster tucked behind your ear. A perfect rose, orchid, or other hothouse flower would be ideal for this. Just wrap the stem in floral tape. You might like to use a smaller matching flower or bud for the groom's boutonniere, with the end similarly wrapped.

A playful gust of wind sweeps back the veil of Julie Olson during her wedding to Tom Taneyhill aboard a sailing ship.

HOW TO MAKE A VEIL

1. Fold tulle into two tiers and round off the corners.

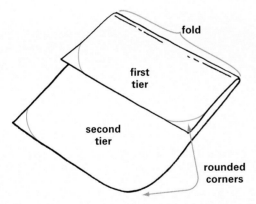

2. Using heavy white thread, sew gathering stitches along the fold line.

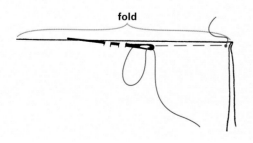

3. Pull up gathering thread as snugly as possible and tie it off securely.

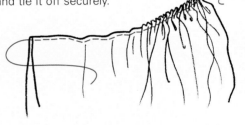

4. Attach the gathered area to a three-inch-wide clear plastic comb or headpiece.

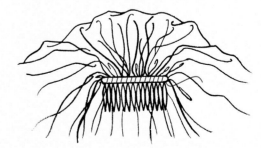

SPECIAL TOUCHES: Add narrow lace or ribbon along outer edges before gathering. Cut apart small lace motifs or small silk flowers and hand-sew them over the veil after gathering.

Some bridesmaids' dresses are just flattering to everybody.

YOUR ATTENDANTS' ATTIRE

A color-coordinated wedding is a work of art. It is especially pleasing to see harmony of dress around a beautiful bride. Elegance and simplicity compliment grace and dignity. The wedding will look more beautiful if all the bridesmaids do, too.

Be daring and dress each bridesmaid to be her loveliest. Buy each a gown in a flattering shade from a single color group, in a style which conceals her figure flaws. You can easily coordinate all your wedding colors with a little study of the floral color wheel on pages 14–15 plus color and fabric swatches.

One way of keeping beauty affordable is to choose simple styles which suit most figures. The outfits may be made distinctive by flowers or by simple and easily made accessories. Formal dresses virtually indistinguishable from designer originals can be bought quite inexpensively at outlet shops or discount department stores. The cost is still lower if they are sewn at home. Remember: Keep it simple and you will achieve elegance.

Maude Lai wed Hoy Chu Don in 1923. The bride (right) and her attendants were a vision of grace and elegance in every detail from gowns to flowers.

There is nothing too lacy, pale, or pretty for a flower girl. Indulge your wildest little girl dreams (and hers!) when you choose her dress.

Find your bridal accessories anywhere you like: a pair of antique kid boots were the timeless inspiration for this bride.

The gentle radiance of an heirloom pearl tiara is repeated again and again in the lovely details of this simple ensemble.

BRIDAL ACCESSORIES

Bridal accessories are more than your grandmother's pearls, a white missal, or gloves. While these treasures are important, utilitarian concerns can make or mar your day.

Someone is bound to cry at your wedding, maybe even you. You don't need a real handbag, but a tiny satin purse to hold a few pretty hankies, lip balm, safety pins, or an aspirin is a good idea. Instructions for our bride's purse can be found on page 80.

Comfortable shoes are essential; you will be on your feet all day. Fancy shoes are fun, but you will do better to find comfortable shoes, leather or fabric. Break them in well, and then decorate them yourself. Hot glue will attach almost anything to a shoe.

If you walk down the aisle in heels, either change to flats for dancing, or become adept at dancing in heels (wearing a long skirt) before the reception. If, after all your efforts, your shoes hurt, kick them off and have the time of your life!

Special Touches

PHOTOGRAPHS, A VIDEO, MUSIC, AND HANDCRAFTED keepsakes enhance the significance and beauty of your wedding ceremony. Underscoring your style and taste, they increase your enjoyment of your special day, now and for years to come.

Music elevates the festivities to something out of the ordinary. It adds a rich texture and an extra layer of emotion, dignity, and magic to the ceremony. For many bridal couples, a wedding without music would feel incomplete.

Photographs preserve the images that make your wedding unique. Years after the event, you and your family, including your future children and grand-children, will enjoy leafing through your wedding album. Pictures help you recall those who shared the day with you, and they are a record of the events of the wedding as well as the small details you may have missed amid the bustle and excitement of the moment.

A videotape records the details—the procession, the exchange of rings, the first kiss—as well as the words and music that make your ceremony complete. Many couples embrace the opportunity to videotape the ceremony because it can speed by like a dream that vanishes before it can be recalled. Small but significant moments deserve to be preserved: the reciting of personally-written vows, a winning smile at a tender moment, a humorous aside by the officiant.

PHOTOGRAPHY

Once you set the wedding date, it's time to choose a photographer: some book a year or more in advance. Look for consistent quality, reliability, and talent, in the photos and the photographer you select.

A wedding specialist is skilled at photographing people under various lighting conditions, under time constraints, and under pressure. He can arrange your gown, show you how to hold the bouquet, and charm the ring bearer into an endearing pose. He will be dealing with nervous people too excited to concentrate, so select one with good "people skills." If you feel comfortable with your photographer, so should your guests.

An experienced professional has at least two portfolios—one of favorite shots and one of a complete wedding. Look for pictures that please you and match your style.

Get a written agreement that includes the number of prints taken, how many formals or candids, who keeps them, who has negatives and printing rights, the cost of reprints, albums, frames, how many hours of coverage you will get, etc. A true professional will give you more information than you asked for.

Think ahead. A parents' album makes a wonderful gift for any occasion.

Ask for help. An experienced photographer can plan the photo session down to the minute, and get the photos you want with smiles to spare.

Consider taking formal and family photos before the ceremony. Families are clustered, everyone is fresh, happy, and enthusiastic. This is also kind to the guests, who want to congratulate you and get down to celebrating.

VIDEOGRAPHY

Should you select a professional videographer or rely on a friend or family member? Professionals know how to work with available lighting, and they have up-to-date equipment and experience. Services such as two-camera

TIPS FOR THE NON-PROFESSIONAL PHOTOGRAPHER

Who better to capture those spontaneous candid, touching, or hilarious photos of you than your family and friends? Here are a few tips to share:

❧ Aim for a mix of posed and informal, candid shots.

❧ Frame your subjects attractively. Look for interesting and beautiful backgrounds. Greenery and handsome architectural details are good choices.

❧ Beware of windows and mirrors; they may reflect flash back to the camera and ruin a perfect shot.

❧ A few long-range shots to recall the setting are nice, but concentrate on well-framed close-ups to capture the intimate joy of wedding moments.

❧ Keep groupings small and close-up.

❧ Avoid using flash during the ceremony; it is intrusive and may be prohibited.

❧ The bride and groom don't see most of what goes on at the wedding; you do. Take photos of what they missed.

work, editing, and special effects will cost more than basic videotaping but provide pleasing results.

❧ Be familiar with any restrictions on videotaping in the sanctuary. Share these with your camera person.

❧ Arrange an interview with the videographer and ask to see examples of his or her work.

❧ Discuss and plan out what you would like to see as the finished product. Your options include raw footage of everything the camera person shoots; a tape edited "in camera," in which the camera person decides what and what not to shoot; a tape that is post-edited, in which some footage is used, other footage discarded, and enhancements such as titles and music may be included; or a tape of highlights alone.

❧ Secure a written agreement that outlines specifically what you will receive, including the quality of the finished videotape.

❧ It is fair to expect the videographer to behave with decorum during the ceremony. Request that he or she avoid interfering with the solemnity of the occasion or your guests' view of the ceremony.

MUSIC FOR THE CEREMONY

Selecting music that will enrich your wedding is an especially joyful task. Your choice of music may be as traditional or personal as you please.

❧ Match music to your theme or style, noting that it need not be grand to be effective. An unaccompanied solo voice or a single guitar can be as moving as a choir or an organist who, literally, pulls out all the stops.

❧ A cappella, instrumental, and accompanied vocal music are all appropriate for weddings.

❧ Wedding music is a vast category, but not all faiths permit all music in the sanctuary. Ask whether your officiant or house of worship has any restrictions against your musical choices. If you want to include a favorite piece not permitted in the ceremony, enjoy it during the reception.

❧ If you know the kind of music you like but are unsure of specific pieces, speak with musicians who perform the

Let the music take you and your guests to wonderful places on your wedding day.

style you like. A soloist or ensemble will suggest pieces from their repertoire that fit the mood of your wedding.

❧ The setting for the music may affect the performance, so along with the music itself you will want to discuss the location with your musicians. Their experience in a similar setting is sure to benefit you.

❧ Besides friends or family members you can turn to for music, some additional resources to consider include a local or regional conservatory or college music department, music stores, orchestras, chamber groups, choirs, and other vocal ensembles. All may have serious musicians happy to perform for a special occasion.

❧ If you yearn for a fully-orchestrated piece but an actual orchestra is impractical, arrange to play a tape or CD of your chosen music. ❧

MEMORY MAKERS

Keepsakes such as a hand-crafted ring bearer's pillow (shown on page 74), flower girl's petal basket (page 80), and bride's purse (page 81) make beautiful finishing touches. These are the flourishes that set this day apart from all others, providing tangible treasures to add to your family's collection of mementos to be handed down and used by future generations. ✺

SATIN RIBBON RING BEARER'S PILLOW

SUPPLIES

7 yards of ¹⁵⁄₁₆"-wide double-faced satin ribbon

⅜ yard satin fabric to match

1¼ yards of ⅜"-wide twisted cord

Four 3½" tassels

2 yards of ¼"-wide satin ribbon

Fiberfill, sewing thread, hot-glue gun

Ribbon rose (see separate instructions; omit leaves)

INSTRUCTIONS

1. Cut two 10" squares of satin fabric.

2. Cut a 10" length of ¹⁵⁄₁₆"-wide ribbon; center it horizontally over one satin square (back) as shown in photo (below left), and baste short ends of ribbon to fabric.

3. Atop remaining satin square (top) weave the ¹⁵⁄₁₆"-wide ribbon diagonally, beginning with longest ribbons (1 & 2

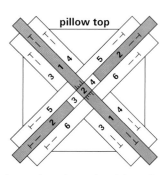

shaded in diagram) laid between corners. Secure ribbons along cut edges of fabric with pins, and trim them to fit the square as you add each ribbon. Continue weaving in order shown in diagram, alternating along the sides of the "X." When fabric is completely covered with weaving, baste ribbon ends ½" from fabric edges and trim ends even with fabric edges.

4. With right sides facing, sew top to back using ½" seam allowance. Leave 3" open for turning. Trim corners, turn right side out, and press lightly. Fill with fiberfill and slip-stitch the opening closed.

5. Tack tassels to pillow corners.

6. Beginning at one corner, hot-glue cord to side seams of pillow; trim cord to fit, gluing raw ends together.

7. Tie ¼"-wide ribbon into a bow measuring 6" across; tack to pillow top as shown in photo. Knot tails of ribbon every 4".

8. Tack underside of ribbon rose to center of pillow top.

A ribbon on the pillow back (left) ensures that little hands will keep a good grip on the pillow during the wedding procession. Decorative ribbon streamers (right) hold the rings in place; a fabric rose will add the crowning touch.

SILK ROSE WITH LEAVES

SUPPLIES

2½ yards of 3"-wide bias-cut silk ribbon for rose

Sewing thread

For optional leaves: 1 yard of 3"-wide bias-cut silk ribbon and 27" length of chenille stem (if necessary, twist shorter stems together snugly to make one continuous length)

Optional pin back

INSTRUCTIONS

1. For the rose, fold back one short end of rose ribbon even with a long edge and sew gathering stitches close to this edge along entire length of ribbon.

2. Pull up gathers as you roll the ribbon from the folded end, tacking gathers every inch or so. To achieve a natural petal shape, sew up to the opposite edge of the ribbon every 12" or so, pulling the thread to gather up the width of the ribbon before continuing to roll and tack the rest of the ribbon length.

3. For optional leaves, twist chenille stem into three connected leaf shapes (see photo) and secure ends at center. Pinch outer edge of each loop into soft points.

4. Cut leaf ribbon into three 12" lengths. On each, fold short ends together, then sew one "side seam" using ⅛" seam allowance. On the other "side seam," secure thread at folded edge and sew gathering stitches through both thicknesses; pull thread to gather seam and secure thread end. Turn leaves right sides out. Gently reshape chenille shape if necessary.

5. Insert a chenille leaf shape into each fabric leaf, and tack together at center. Gently reshape chenille shape if necessary.

6. Tack bottom of rose to center of leaf cluster (gathered seams up).

7. If making a pin, sew pin back to underside of leaf cluster at center.

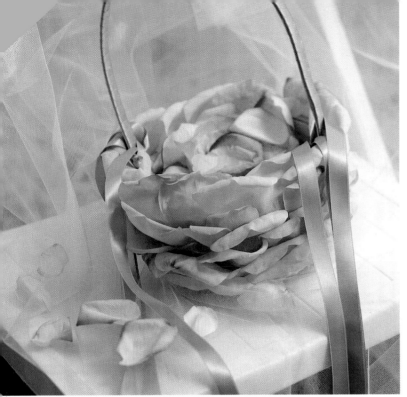

Lustrous silk petals and streamers make a flower girl's simple basket into a bouquet.

FLOWER GIRL'S PETAL BASKET

SUPPLIES

Round basket of your choice with handle, approx. 3½"
   high x 7" in diameter

3–4 artificial roses, 5"-6" blooms in color of your choice

5–6 yards of ⅝"-wide double-faced satin ribbon to coordinate with flowers

Hot glue

INSTRUCTIONS

1. Remove the individual petals from the roses by pulling or cutting them off with scissors.

2. When you hot-glue the petals to the basket, work in rows. Start at the top using the larger petals. Use smaller petals as you work your way down, with the very smallest petals in the bottom row.

3. Starting with the first row, overlap each petal in the same direction. An overlap of half of the previous petal is about right, but this may vary with different rose petals. The first row of petals should extend well above the top of the basket (⅔ of the petal).

4. The second row of petals should overlap about half of the previous row. Glue petals in the opposite direction and offset from the previous row (like bricks).

5. Wrap the handle with ⅝"-wide satin ribbon, trailing 12"-18" of extra ribbon down each side. Tie a 1-yard length of ribbon at each handle to give you a total of three trailing ribbons.

6. Hot-glue ribbon around the bottom of the basket, covering the edge of the last row of petals.

SATIN-RIBBON BRIDE'S PURSE

SUPPLIES

10 yards of ¹⁵⁄₁₆"-wide double-faced white satin ribbon

¼ yard of white satin fabric

¾ yard of ⅛"-wide white twisted cord

Two 3½"-long white tassels

White sewing thread

INSTRUCTIONS

1. Cut two 6" x 15" rectangles of satin fabric. Atop one piece (face), weave ribbons diagonally one at a time, beginning at center (see Step 3, page 78). Pin ribbon along cut edges of fabric and trim to fit rectangle. When fabric is completely covered with weaving, baste ribbon ends ½" from fabric edges.

2. With right sides facing, fold short edges of face piece together and sew side seams, using ½" seam allowance; allow scant ⅛" gaps at fold (into which you'll tuck cord and tassel later). Trim corners, turn right side out, and press lightly.

3. Sew side seams of remaining rectangle (lining), leaving a 3" opening for turning.

4. Slip face inside lining and sew along top edges (½" seam allowance). Turn right side out through opening in lining; slip-stitch opening, and tuck lining into bag.

5. Beginning at one lower corner and tucking ends of cord into gaps in side seams, slip-stitch cord to side seams of bag, forming a handle.

6. Attach tassels to lower corners, tucking hangers into gaps in side seams.

Celebrating the Newlyweds

WEDDINGS ARE ROMANTIC NEW BEGINNINGS, AND AS SUCH deserve the joyful acknowledgment of the gathered guests. Once vows are spoken and the union officially pronounced, those assembled may offer a tribute to the bride and groom, showering them symbolically with warmest wishes for their future life together. For generations, handfuls of uncooked rice, signifying fertility, were happily tossed by the guests. Today rice is out of favor, replaced by a variety of fanciful, elegant, sometimes playful "wishes." A bliss of bubbles, a blessing of birdseed, a rhapsody of ringing bells, a praise of petals all make an exuberant salute to the bride and groom. Which will you choose?

Invite your family and friends to join you in a get-together or favor party, to assemble the "send-off" favors presented in the next pages. ✑

Tuck birdseed into floral teabag packets for guests to shower the
newlyweds after the ceremony. Construct them of pretty wrapping
paper that echoes the colors of the wedding.

BIRDSEED PACKETS

SUPPLIES FOR EACH PACKET

8" x 7" rectangle of wrapping paper

4" of narrow silk ribbon

One small silk rosette or other flower

2 tsp. of birdseed (roast in oven for 10 min. at 350° to
 prevent germination)

Glue stick, double-stick tape, a hot glue gun

CONSTRUCTION

1. Fold and crease one 8" side of the paper 2¼" from the left edge. Fold and crease the right edge so folded paper is now 2½" x 8" wide (photo shows the inside).

2. To make the teabag shape, fold outer sides of the paper together in half, making a horizontal crease. Make parallel folds ¼" away, folding in the opposite direction.

3. Open the paper and apply glue stick along the horizontal creases. Refold the left edge and apply glue stick inside the right edge. Refold into teabag shape.

4. Fold and crease corners of top edge (inner flap) so they meet. Fold and crease corners of bottom edge (outer flap) ¼" apart.

5. Unfold flaps and fill each side of packet with 1 tsp. birdseed.

6. Refold with outer flap on outside of packet and hold it in place with a small square of double-stick tape.

7. Loop ribbon in half and attach to point of flap, using a hot glue gun. Glue rosette atop ribbon loop.

Pressed-flower-petal holders attached to chairs at an outdoor wedding allow guests to shower the newlyweds during the recessional.

PRESSED-FLOWER-PETAL HOLDER

SUPPLIES FOR EACH PETAL HOLDER

Approximately 12 rose petals

Two 8" x 9" sheets of waxed paper

Transparent tape

Double-stick tape

30" of rayon hem tape

22" of 2"-wide sheer ribbon

Pattern drawn on graph paper

Scalloped-edge scissors

CONSTRUCTION

1. Press petals in a flower press or between the pages of a book; allow one week to dry.

2. Place petals between sheets of waxed paper and press with iron set on low temperature until wax melts enough to bond the sheets.

3. Trim waxed paper to match the pattern, using scalloped-edge scissors on the curved edge.

4. Place hem tape atop waxed paper, then fold paper into a cone shape and secure with an inch of transparent tape on the outside just above the bottom point.

5. Tie ends of hem tape together in a knot and gently pull knot to inside point of cone.

6. To make the hanger, join hem tape together just above the edge of the paper, using a small piece of double-stick tape.

7. Tie sheer ribbon into a bow around the base of the hanger.

8. Fill with fresh petals and hang on chair backs.

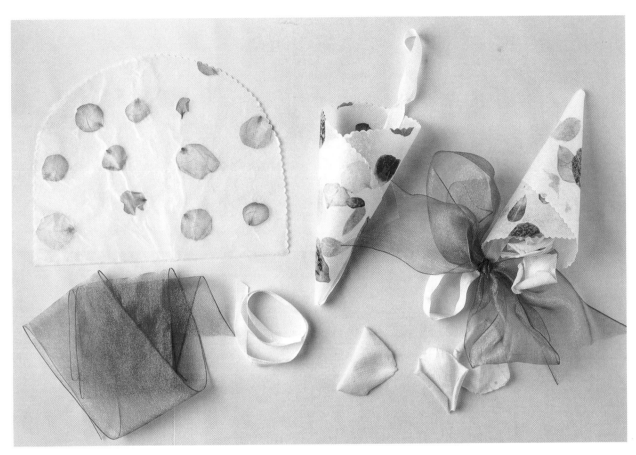

Create translucent cones with dried rose petals pressed between two sheets of waxed paper. A loop of hem tape makes into a handle that can be easily tied to each chair with a sheer ribbon bow.

A garland of wispy, rose-petalled tulle drapes from chair to chair along the ceremony aisle. First, glue rose petals sparsely to the front of the tulle, then glue to the opposite side, matching petal-to-petal for the perfect finishing touch.

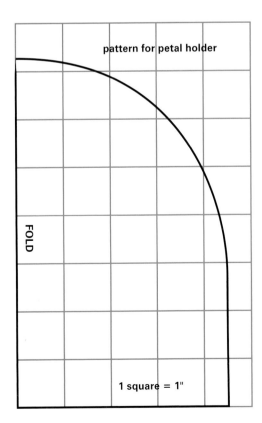

pattern for petal holder

FOLD

1 square = 1"

Guests greet the newlyweds with a shower of bubbles.

Bubbles capture the effervescence of the happy moment, putting your guests in a playful mood. Purchase simple plastic bubble bottles at a party favor store, then add your own embellishments using glue: ribbons and bows, rosettes and leaves, faux jewels, even a champagne "spray" of pearls on wire.

Releasing white doves—actually homing pigeons trained to return to their keeper—provides a dramatic post-ceremony event, expressing the soaring hopes of, and for, the bridal couple.

RESOURCES

CALLIGRAPHY

George Spindler Design
333 N. McDowell Blvd. #A333
Petaluma, CA 94954
tel 707-766-6009

DRESSMAKER

Jean Elliott
704 Bloomfield Rd.
Sebastopol, CA 95472

FLOWERS

IMPRESSIONS FLORAL DESIGN GALLERIA

2 Theatre Square, #136
Orinda, CA 94563-3346
tel 925-253-0250
fax 925-253-9946

INVITATIONS

PRINTED AFFAIR

Leslie Bond, Marcia Redford
460 Boulevard Way
Oakland, CA 94610
tel 510-654-9903
fax 510-654-9916

LOCATIONS

JEFFERSON STREET MANSION

Reed Robbins
tel 707-746-0684
fax 707-746-1639
www.mansions-cuisine.com

RIBBON

MIDORI INC.

708 6th Ave.
Seattle, WA 98109
Wholesale only; call for a store
near you.
tel 206-282-3595
fax 206-282-3431
www.midoriribbon.com

WEDDING GOWNS

SHADOWS

Jean and Charles Stewart
New and vintage bridal wear
429 San Anselmo Ave.
San Anselmo, CA 94960
tel 415-459-0574
fax 415-459-0465
www.shadowsjewelry.com

PHOTO CREDITS

We offer our special thanks to Dianne Woods and to Don Fraser, whose dedication to the art of photography created the incomparable photographs in this book.

Additionally, we want to extend a special thank you to the many brides and grooms whose inspiring images grace our pages.

DIANE WOODS
1041 Folger St., Berkeley, CA 94710; 510-841-9220
FRONT AND BACK COVERS,
PAGES: 5 (third & fourth from top), 6, 8 (right), 17 (bottom), 18, 19, 20, 21, 22, 31, 33, 36 (top & bottom left), 37, 38, 42, 43, 44 (bottom), 45, 46, 47, 51, 52, 53, 67 (right), 72, 74, 75, 78, 79, 80, 81, 84, 85, 86, 87, 88 (bottom)

DON FRASER
1041 Folger St., Berkeley, CA 94710; 510-704-1849
PAGE 4: Teri Thompson and John O'Neal, Valley Presbyterian Church, Portola Valley, CA
PAGE 5: (top) Julie Skidmore and John Lewman, Fremont, CA; (2nd from top) Jennifer Renner and Joe Pezzolo, St. Dominic's Church, San Francisco, CA
PAGE 8: Victoria Littlejohn and Eric Schoenke, St. Clemen's Church, Berkeley, CA
PAGE 9: (left) Heather Dickinson and Grant Fondo, Meadowood Country Club, St. Helena, CA; (right) Kerry Clark and Richard Spindler, Auberge du Soleil Restaurant, Rutherford, CA
PAGE 10: Heather Dickinson and Grant Fondo, Meadowood Country Club, St. Helena, CA
PAGE 11: Gerry Dale and Randal Bauman, Tilden Park Brazilian Room, Berkeley, CA
PAGE 12: Stacy Baker and Todd Morris, Old Marsh Creek Springs, Clayton, CA
PAGE 13: (top left) Nancy St. Clair and Nick Iacobitti, Northbrae Community Church, Berkeley, CA; (top right) Stacey Getz and Robert Kertsman, Lark Creek Inn, Larkspur, CA; (bottom left) Tomiko Iwata and Keith Silverton, Mill Valley Outdoor Art Club, Mill Valley, CA; (bottom right) Ann Goforth and Jim Henderson, Sausalito Women's Club, Sausalito, CA

PAGE 16: Mary Jane Pasha and Thomas Maxstadt, St. Leo's Church, Boyes Hot Spring, CA
PAGE 24: Stacy Baker and Todd Morris, Old Marsh Creek Springs, Clayton, CA
PAGE 25: Old St. Hillary's Church, Tiburon, CA
PAGE 26: Janelle Pieri and David Glenn, Grace Cathedral, San Francisco, CA
PAGE 27: Melissa Chamberlain and Ken Leet, Clos Pegase Winery, St. Helena, CA
PAGE 28: (bottom) Shawn Elliott and Jack Marshall, Beaulieu Gardens, Rutherford, CA
PAGE 29: (bottom) Mia Senior and Chris Untermann, private residence, San Rafael, CA
PAGE 30: Sibyl Otter and David Kaufman, Bohemian Club, San Francisco, CA
PAGE 34: Jennifer Nutting and William Blandón, S.F. Yacht Club, San Francisco, CA
PAGE 35: (left) Lynn Robie and Geoff Zimmerman, Captain Walsh House, Benicia, CA
PAGE 40: (left) Stacey Getz and Robert Kertsman, Lark Creek Inn, Larkspur, CA; (right) Lyn Tallarida and Joe Gatti, St. Raphael's Church, San Rafael, CA
PAGE 41: Laura Simmons and Scot Boland, Hacienda de las Flores, Moraga, CA
PAGE 44: Cara Trautvetter and Clayton Cieslak, private residence, Pinole, CA
PAGE 48: (top left & right) Joanne Lehrer (bottom left) Diana Loo and Ted Chan, Thomas Fogarty Vineyards, Woodside, CA
PAGE 49: Jennifer Nutting and Wiliam Blandón, S.F. Yacht Club, San Francisco, CA
PAGE 50: Mary Jane Pasha and Thomas Maxstadt, St. Leo's Church, Boyes Hot Springs, CA
PAGE 54: Lynn Robie and Geoff Zimmerman, Captain Walsh House, Benicia, CA
PAGE 55: Laura Simmons and Scot Boland, Hacienda de las Flores, Moraga, CA
PAGE 56: Lyn Tallarida and Joe Gatti, St. Raphael's Church, San Rafael, CA
PAGE 57: Melissa Jue and Matthew Steeves, Westminster Presbyterian Church, Tiburon, CA
PAGE 58: (left) Janice Johnson and Thomas Savidge, City Club, San Francisco, CA; (right) Jennifer Renner and Joe Pezzolo, World Trade Club, San Francisco, CA
PAGE 59: Kate Crane and Milan Smith, Domain Carneros Winery, Napa Valley, CA
PAGE 63: Pamela Meyer and David Dresher, Hamlin School, San Francisco, CA

Page 64 & 65: Dorene Kruspe, Joanne Lehrer
PAGE 68: (left) Jennifer Renner and Joe Pezzolo, private home, San Francisco, CA; (right) Julie Skidmore and John Lewman, Fremont, CA
PAGE 70: Shawn Elliott and Jack Marshall, Beaulieu Gardens, Rutherford, CA
PAGE 71: Laura Simmons and Scot Boland, Hacienda de las Flores, Moraga, CA
PAGE 73: (left) Laura Simmons and Scot Boland, Hacienda de las Flores, Moraga, CA; (right) Rose Cardinale and Salvatore Ingrande, private residence, San Mateo, CA
PAGE 77: Baquette Quartette at the wedding of Ann Goforth and Jim Henderson, Sausalito Women's Club, Sausalito, CA
PAGE 82: Lyn Tallarida and Joe Gatti, St. Raphael's Church, San Rafael, CA
PAGE 83: Jennifer Renner and Joe Pezzolo, St. Dominic's Church, San Francisco, CA
PAGE 88: (top) Anna-Marie Shinall and Chris Berry, Preservation Park, Oakland, CA
PAGE 89: Nobuko Mukai and John Vicars, Mira Vista Country Club, El Cerrito, CA
PAGE 95: Lyn Tallarida and Joe Gatti, St. Rafael's Church, San Rafael, CA

DAVID SPINDLER
Spindler Photography, 801 22nd Street, San Francisco, CA 94107, 415-285-4367
PAGE 22: Engagement photo of Shannon Gallagher and Don Hall

DAN CATHERWOOD
Christopher Kight Photographers, 2638 El Paseo Lane, Town & Country Village, Sacramento, CA 95821; 916-484-1164
PAGE 28-29: Karen Janes and Craig Coane, Cathedral of the Blessed Sacrament, Sacramento, CA

UNKNOWN PHOTOGRAPHER
Page 35: Joanne Simon and David Main, private residence, Lafayette, CA

KATHLEEN AHERN
Ahern Photography, 2155 Las Positas Court, Suite C, Livermore, CA 94550; 925-606-8800

Page 36: Leslie Johnson and Phillip Altman, Heather Farms, Walnut Creek, CA

STEPHANIE TABACHNIKOFF
510-632-5886
Page 62: Basha Kooler and Mark Hanner, Grandma's Bed and Breakfast, Berkeley, CA

JEFF LAMBERTSON
Danville, CA, friend of the groom
Page 69: Julie Olson and Tom Taneyhill on the sailing ship Balclutha, San Francisco, CA

Index

A .... Accessories, for the bride 72-73
　　　　　See also Jewelry, Keepsakes
　　Attire
　　　　for attendants 70-71
　　　　for bride 57-69
　　　　See also Gowns

B .... Basket for flower girl, how to make 80
　　Beaches 28
　　Bouquet(s) 38-55
　　　　alternatives to 48
　　　　bridal 40-51
　　　　herbs for 44
　　　　mixed 44
　　　　single flower 40-41
　　　　using callas 46-47
　　　　See also Flowers
　　Boutonniere 40, 49, 52, 54
　　Bow(s), *See* Ribbons
　　Breakfast 8
　　Bridesmaids' dresses 70
　　Buddhist 13
　　Budget 7, 8, 16, 23, 35, 39

C .... Calla bouquet, how to make 46-47
　　Calligraphy 17, 19
　　Cathedral 26
　　Catholic 12
　　Ceremony, style of 11-13
　　Chapel 26
　　Children 17
　　Chinese 12
　　Christian 13
　　Church 26, 29
　　Club 26
　　Color(s) 14-15
　　　　in gowns 59
　　　　See also Flowers
　　Computer-aided design, for invitations 19, 23
　　Consultant, wedding 16
　　Corsages 49, 52, 53
　　Customs, wedding 12

D .... Decorations
　　　　for ceremony 31-37
　　　　using flowers 31, 33, 34, 37
　　　　using ribbons 36, 37, 87
　　　　using tulle 31, 36, 37, 87
　　　　See also Flowers
　　Dinner 8

E .... Expression, personal 8

F .... Favors 83-88
　　　　birdseed packets 84-85
　　　　bubbles 88
　　　　pressed-flower petal holders 86-87
　　Fees 26, 28
　　Florist, working with 49
　　Flower girl 71
　　Flowers 30-55
　　　　as hair ornaments 48, 69
　　　　boutonniere(s) 40, 52, 54
　　　　budgeting for 35, 49
　　　　calla bouquet 46-47
　　　　caring for (conditioning) 55
　　　　corsages 52-53
　　　　decorating with 31, 33, 34, 37
　　　　for bride 39, 40, 48, 69
　　　　for bridesmaids 40
　　　　for door 33
　　　　for indoor ceremonies 31
　　　　for mantel 31
　　　　for reception 35
　　　　for time of day 42
　　　　fragrance 40
　　　　in relation to gown 58
　　　　mixed bouquets 44
　　　　potted plants 35, 37
　　　　pressed, for favors 86-87
　　　　seasonal 42, 50
　　　　selecting 42, 49
　　　　symbolism of 31, 44, 45
　　　　See also Florist

G Gardens 28, 35
Gift(s) 8
Gown(s) 57-71
    back(s) of 62
    balancing flowers with 58
    colors of 59
    dressmaking terms for 60-63
    from bridal salon 63
    make your own 64-65
    seasonal considerations 58
    selecting with a dressmaker or salesperson 65
    styles of 57, 60-61
    used or period 59, 63
    non-traditional 59
    sources for 59, 63
    See also Attire

H Hand lettering, on invitations. *See* Calligraphy
Headpiece(s) for the bride 48, 68-69
Herbs, in bouquets. 44
    See also Flowers
Heritage 12
Historic home 28
Hotel 26

I Inn 28
Invitations 18-23
    budgeting for 23
    computer-aided design of 19, 23
    embossing 23
    enclosures 21, 23
    ordering 23
    when to mail 20
    wording 20, 23

J Jewelry 17, 62, 73
    See also Accessories
Jewish 12, 13

K Keepsakes 75, 78-81

L Locations, *See also* Site(s)

M Maps 20
Music 8, 17, 75, 77

O Orthodox, Russian 12
Outdoor ceremonies 25, 26, 28, 29, 34, 35, 40

P Parks 28
Personal touches 17
Pet(s) 17
Photography 75-76
Pillow, ring bearer's, how to make 78-79
Planning 7-9, 11, 15, 16
Purse, bride's, how to make 80-81

R Reception cards 20, 21
Recreation areas 28
Regulations and restrictions 26, 58, 77
Residence 26
Response (return) cards 20, 21
Restaurants 26
Ribbon(s) 36, 37, 48
    bows, how to tie 32
    bride's purse 80-81
    in flower-petal basket 80
    rose with leaves, how to make 79
    woven into pillow 78-79
    wrapping for floral stems 46-47
Rituals 12
    See also Traditions

S Season of the year 8, 28, 42, 50
Settings, *See also* Site(s)
Sites 8, 25-35
    considerations that influence choice 25
    decorating 17, 26
    indoor 26, 28, 31
    outdoor 25, 28, 35
Stamps 17
Synagogue 26

T Time of day 8, 28, 42
Tradition(s) 12, 70, 83
    See also Rituals

U Unity Candle 12

V Veil(s),
    bridal 68
    how to make 68-69
Videography 75-77
Vows 12

W Wineries 28
Wreath 33

the beginning . . .